COLOR THRU HISTORY

THE PEOPLE OF THE MODERN AGE

PICTURE BOOK SUPPLEMENT

Learn & Color Books
 an imprint of Master Design Marketing, LLC
 30 N Gould St, Ste R
 Sheridan, WY 82801
 www.LearnAndColor.com

For information about special discounts available for bulk purchases, sales promotions, fund-raising and educational needs, contact Learn & Color Books Company Sales at sales@LearnAndColor.com.

ISBN: 978-1-947482-55-5 (paperback)
ISBN: 978-1-947482-56-2 (hardback)
ISBN: 978-1-947482-57-9 (ebook)

Cover and interior design by Faithe F Thomas
Research by Caitlyn F Williams
Images are © Master Design Marketing, LLC

Look for the Scottish Flag somewhere in each of our books.

Henry Ford was an American who founded of the Ford Motor Company. He developed the assembly line technique of mass production.

Marie Curie was a Polish and French scientist who researched radioactivity and invented mobile X-ray units.

Mohandas Gandhi led India to independence from British colonial rule and inspired movements for civil rights across the world.

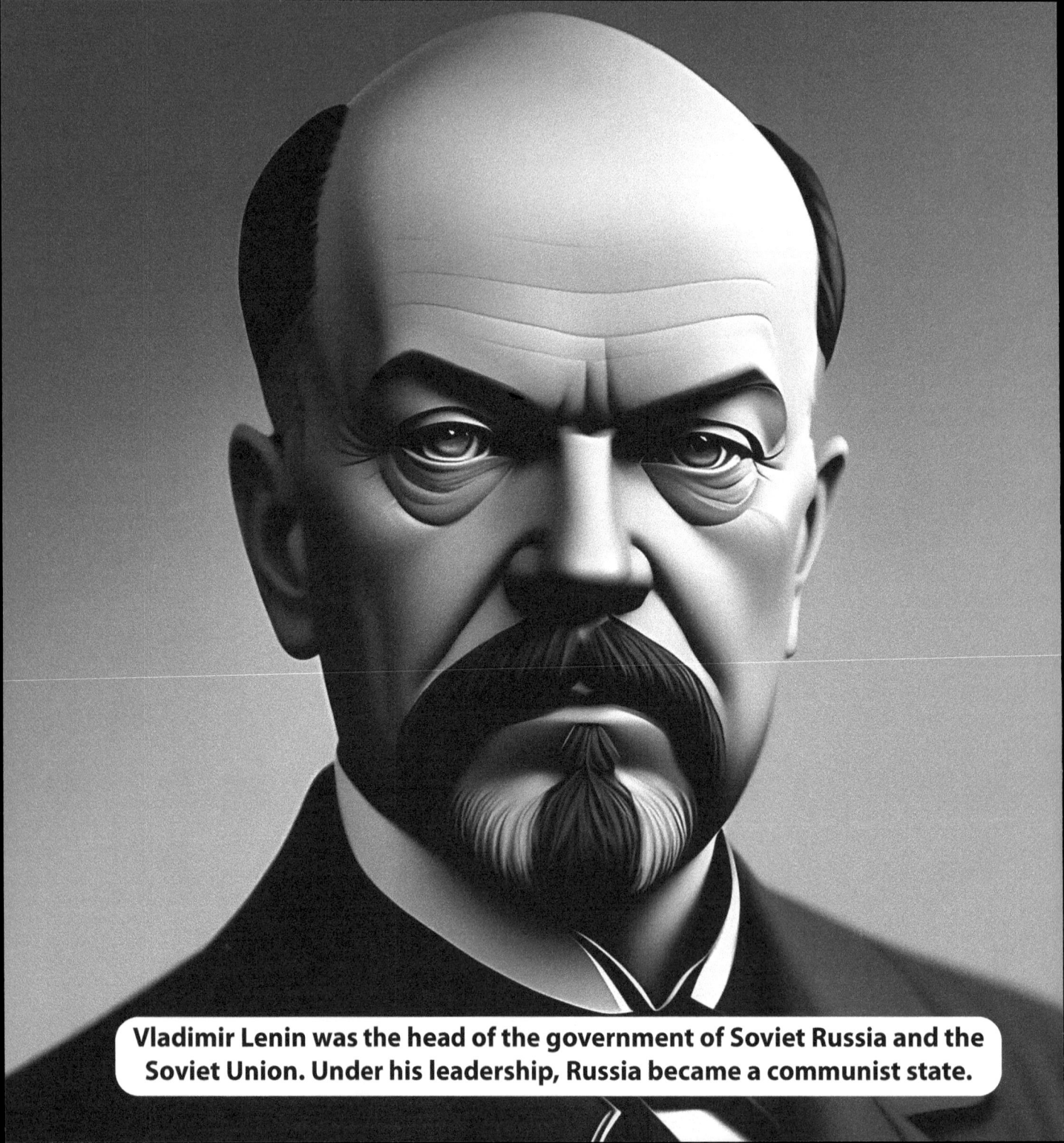
Vladimir Lenin was the head of the government of Soviet Russia and the Soviet Union. Under his leadership, Russia became a communist state.

Sir Winston Churchill was Prime Minister of the United Kingdom when he led Britain to victory in WWII.

Joseph Stalin led the Soviet Union (USSR).

Albert Einstein was a German genius.
He is best known for his formula: $E = mc^2$.

Helen Keller was an American author and lecturer. She was the first deaf-blind person to earn a Bachelor of Arts degree.

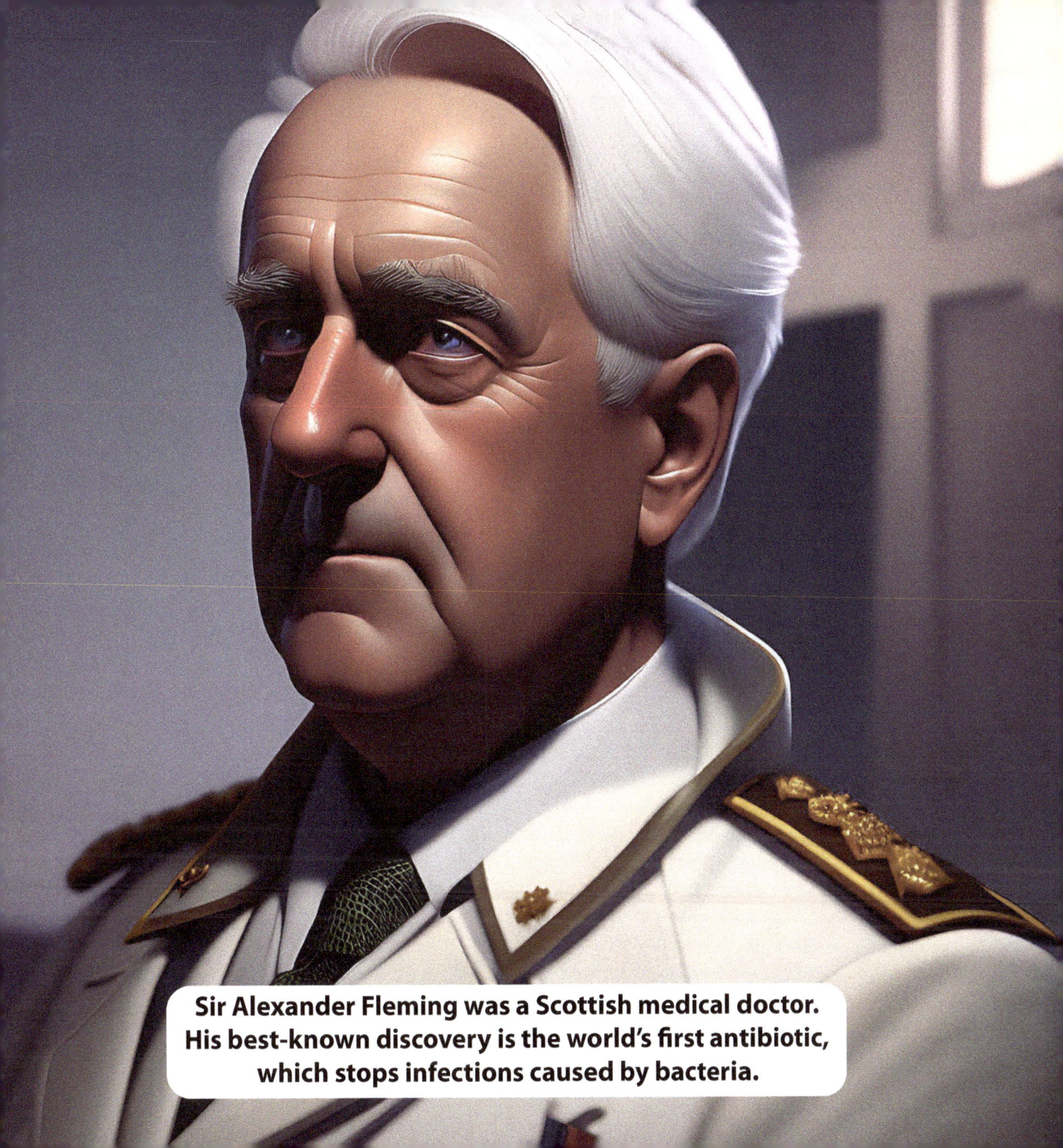

Sir Alexander Fleming was a Scottish medical doctor. His best-known discovery is the world's first antibiotic, which stops infections caused by bacteria.

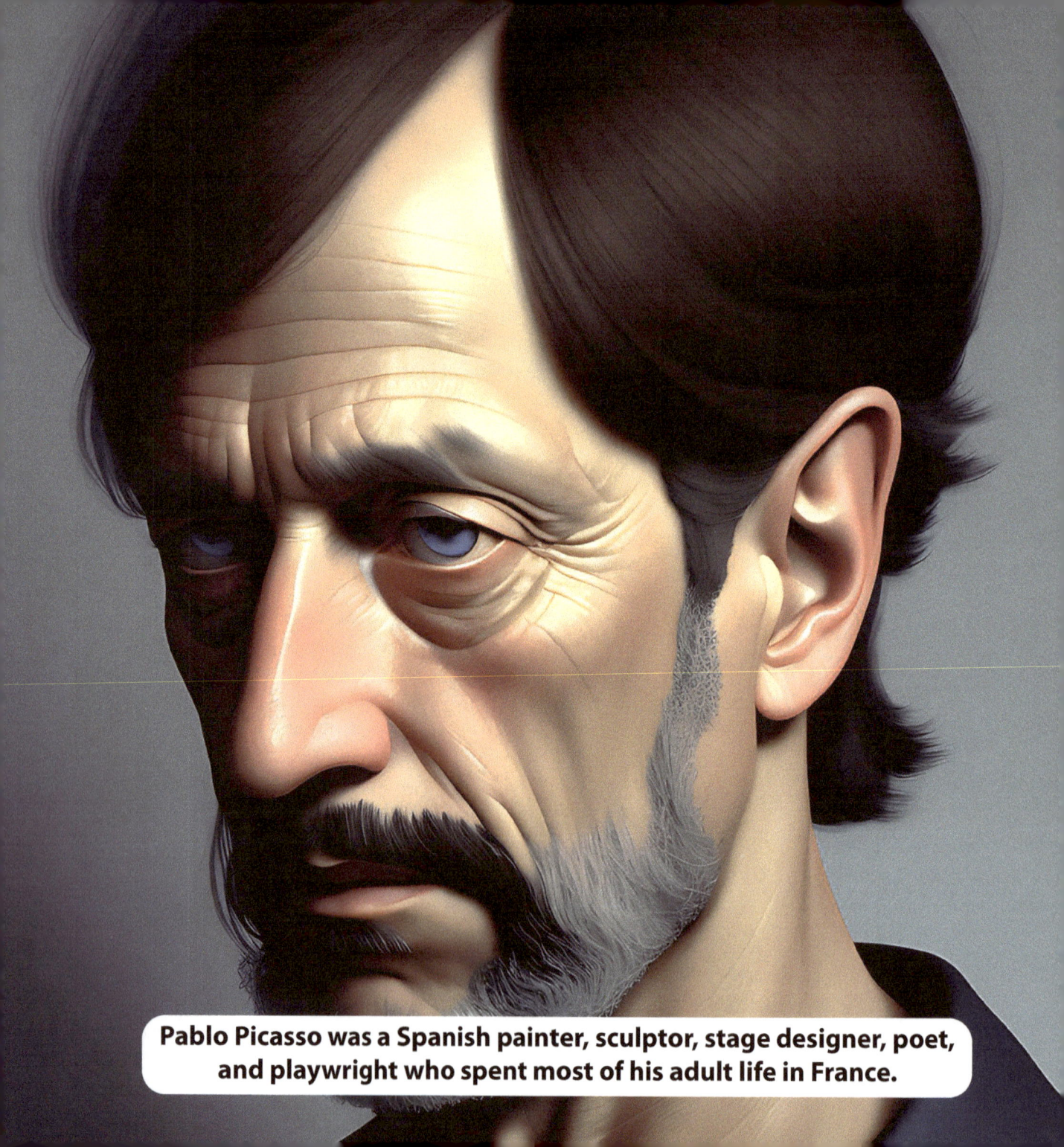
Pablo Picasso was a Spanish painter, sculptor, stage designer, poet, and playwright who spent most of his adult life in France.

Franklin Delano Roosevelt was the only president of the United States to serve more than two terms. He was the president during World War II.

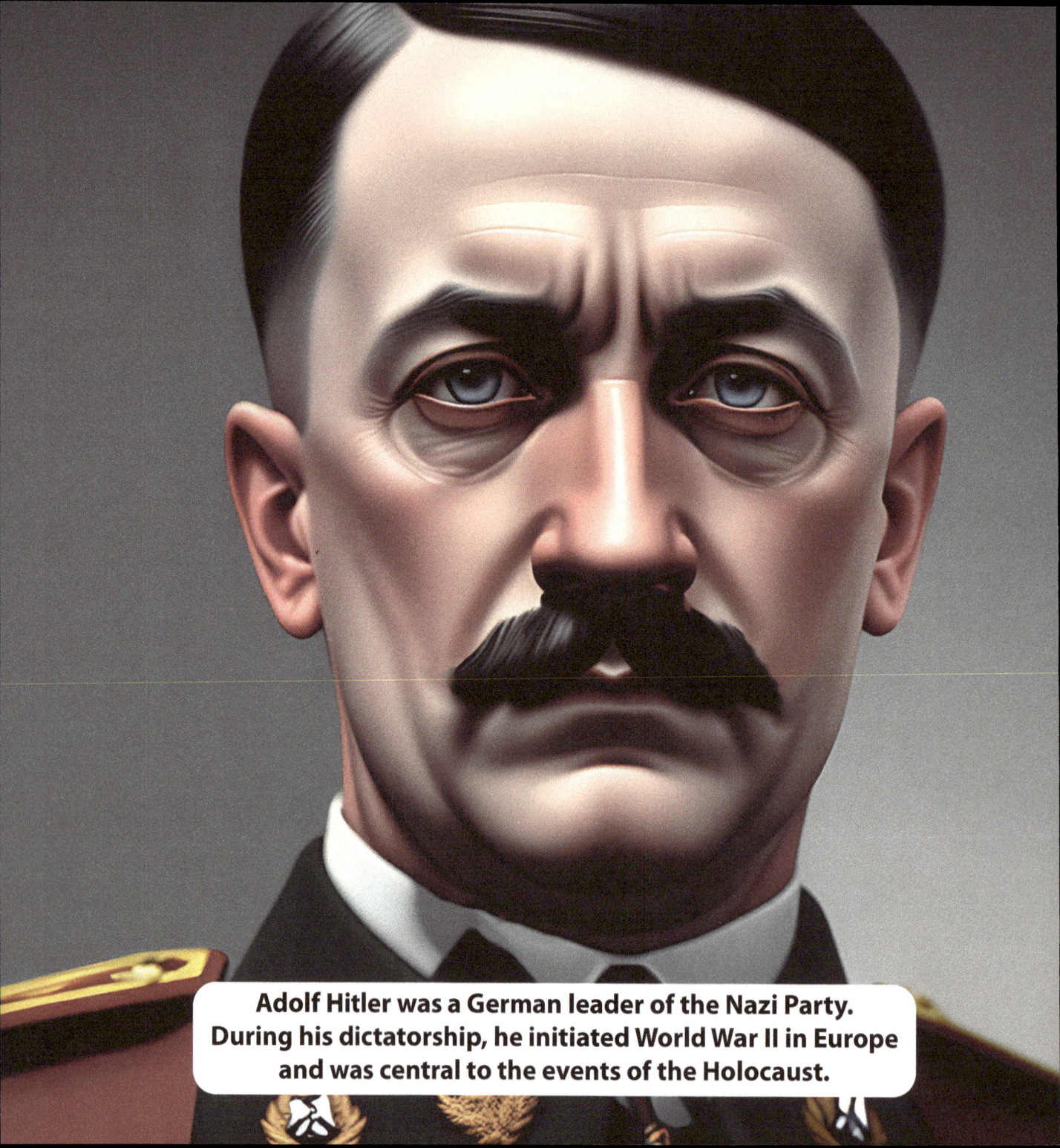

Adolf Hitler was a German leader of the Nazi Party. During his dictatorship, he initiated World War II in Europe and was central to the events of the Holocaust.

Charles de Gaulle was a French statesman who led the French Resistance against Nazi Germany in World War II.

Mao Zedong was a Chinese communist revolutionary who became the founding father of the People's Republic of China.

Walt Disney was the creator of the Walt Disney entertainment empire, which includes the Disney theme parks.

George Orwell was an English author who wrote books about society and governments.

Julius Robert Oppenheimer was an American scientist who was the "father of the atomic bomb."

Salvador Dali was a prominent Spanish painter. He was best known for the striking and bizarre images in his works.

Mother Teresa started schools in India run by volunteers to educate street children and run soup kitchens as well as other services.

Lucille Ball was an American actress, comedian, model, and producer. She was the first female studio executive.

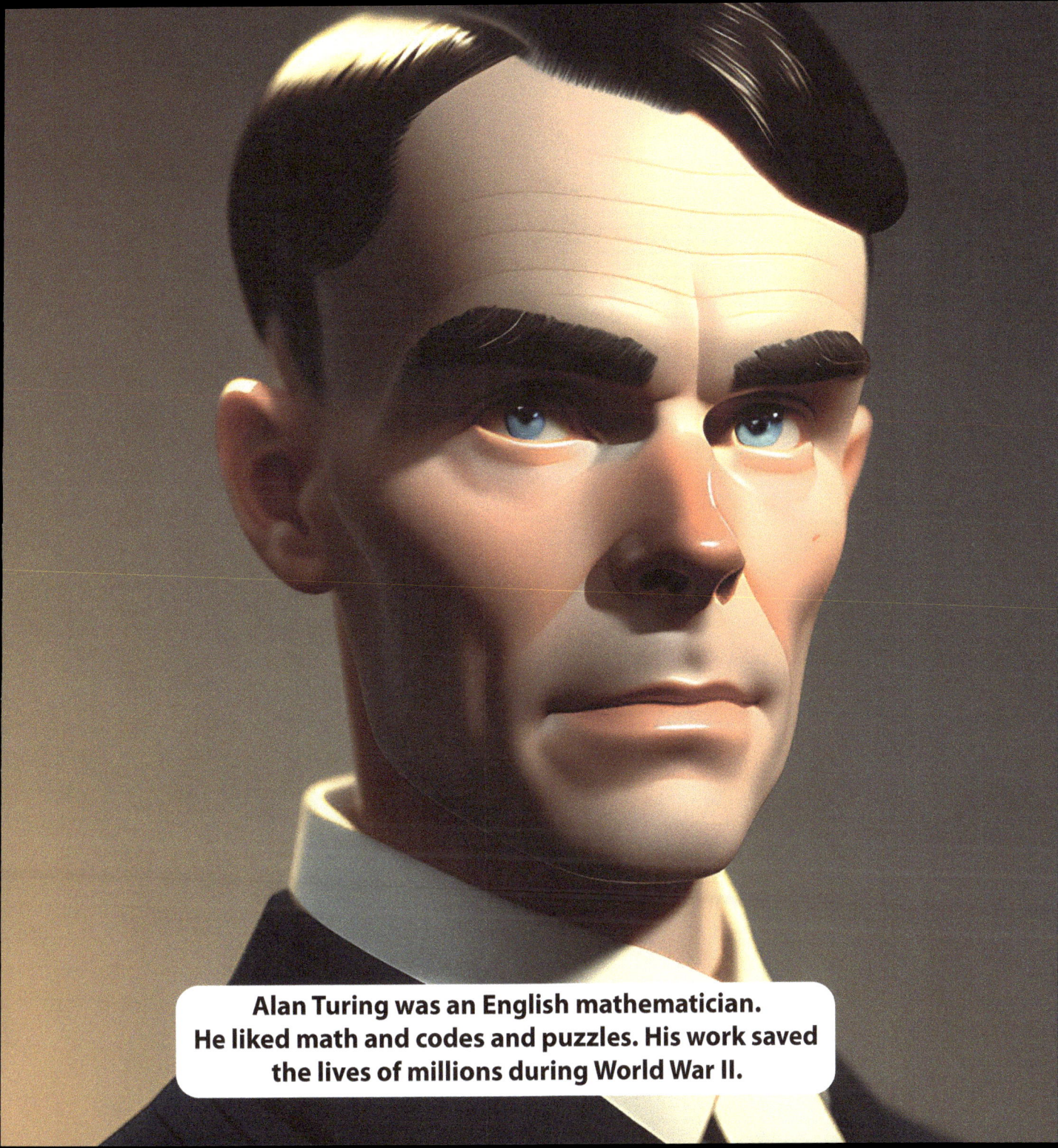

Alan Turing was an English mathematician.
He liked math and codes and puzzles. His work saved
the lives of millions during World War II.

Rosa Parks was an American activist in the civil rights movement.
She has been called "the first lady of civil rights"
and "the mother of the freedom movement."

John F. Kennedy was the youngest man to be elected as U.S. president.

Nelson Mandela was president of South Africa.
He fought racism and brought about reconcilliation.

Billy Graham was a prominent evangelical Christian figure. He was a spiritual adviser to U.S. presidents from the 33rd, Harry S. Truman, to the 44th, Barack Obama.

Elie Wiesel was a Romanian-born American writer, professor, and Holocaust survivor. He was a Jewish prisoner in the Auschwitz and Buchenwald concentration camps during World War II.

Anne Frank was a German-born Dutch-Jew.
She is one of the most discussed Jewish victims of the
Holocaust due to her diary, which survived the war.

Martin Luther King Jr. was an American Baptist minister and activist who became the most visible spokesperson and leader in the civil rights movement.

Elvis Presley was an American singer, musician, and actor. He is often referred to as the "King of Rock and Roll."

John Lennon was an English singer, songwriter, and peace activist who co-founded the Beatles, the most commercially successful band in the history of popular music.